Contents

*Brooklands School,
Greenwich, London 1958*

New schools

Albrighton School, Shropshire

After the end of the Second World War, many new babies were born.
It was called a "baby boom". By 1950, these children were old enough
to go to school. More schools were needed. New schools were built
on new housing estates and in New Towns.

**"Our school was only one of five new schools built at that time.
It was part of a big building programme."**

Look at the school in the photograph.

Look for:

—the flat roof
—the large windows
—the builder's plank by the main entrance.

**"I was one of the first pupils at the school.
I remember the day it opened for the first time."**

This photograph shows
a crowded school hall.
Look at the children
and visitors. They are
there for the opening
of a new school. Can
you see the mayor?

Forster School, Lewisham, London 1952

Things to do

Start to make a book about schools in the 1950s. Call the first page *New Schools*.
Find a school near where you live, like the ones in the photographs.
Draw a picture or take a photograph of it. Try to find someone who can
tell you about when a school opened. Write down what they tell you.

If your school is an old school, look carefully round the building.
Were any new parts built in the 1950s?

Inside school

Kingswood School, Basildon, Essex 1957

**"The school was light and airy.
All round it was green grass and garden.
I had never taught in such a marvellous building before."**

Here is a photograph of
the teachers at a school
30 years ago. Notice
that the women teachers
are not wearing trousers.

St Francis de Sales School, London

The new schools had extra rooms that older schools did not have.

"We had a large central hall, inside lavatories, a staff room, kitchen and dining room."

Look at this photograph of children reading in their classroom. Working in small groups was a new idea in the 1950s.

Essendon School, Hertfordshire 1949

Things to do

Talk to a teacher who worked in an old school but moved to a new school. What was different about the new school? Write down what they tell you in your book.

Draw a plan of your school. Write on it the names of each room.

The classroom

Upper Tulse Hill School, London 1952

Here is a class of boys in their new classroom.

Look for:

— the large windows

— the desks with a shelf underneath, arranged in rows

— the handwriting exercise on the blackboard.

— the loudspeaker on the wall in the photograph.

Sometimes the children listened to Schools Radio programmes.

"The master radio was in the office.

There were speakers in every room.

You plugged in in your classroom if you wanted to listen."

"The ballpoint pen had just come in. It was the end of the old pen and ink."

These older girls had locker desks. They were new in the 1950s.

Dee House Ursuline Convent School, Chester 1956

"Mine was always untidy. It was so nice to have somewhere to keep all our things."

Things to do

Look round your school. What sort of desks do you have? How are they arranged? Is it the same or different from the 1950s?

Ask your head teacher if there are any photographs like these of your school.

Draw a picture of a new classroom in the 1950s.

School clothes

All Saints School, Farnworth, Lancashire 1954

These children went to an old school in 1954. It has now been pulled down.

Look for:

— the boys in short trousers
— the girls in skirts with straps
— the short hair cuts of the boys
— the girls' hair tied with ribbon
— the children with National Health glasses.

**"I loved to choose my hair ribbon each morning.
I matched the colour to the rest of my clothes.
Under our skirts we wore navy blue knickers."**

Some schools had a uniform.
The children wore a school tie
and a school badge on their
blazer pocket. Look at the girl
in her school uniform.

**"We didn't insist on it, but they
could wear it if they liked."**

Things to do

In your book write the heading *School clothes*.
Look at what your teachers and other children in your class
wear to school. How have things changed since the 1950s?
Draw some pictures and write about what you notice.

Collect some old school photographs. Compare them with
a photograph of your class now.

Find out about the National Health Service.

School milk

Every child was given
a free bottle of milk
each day. At playtime
the milk and straws
were given out.

"I liked being
the milk monitor.
I had to put the
straws in the bottles.
We saved the milk
tops to buy guide
dogs for the blind."

Deansfield School, London 1963

10

Many new school kitchens were built in the 1950s. Dinners were cooked for other schools in the neighbourhood.

"We all had a hot dinner served through the hatch. At half past eleven each day, a van drew up. It took meals from our kitchen in containers to other people."

Caldecot School, Denmark Hill, London 1951

Things to do

Write the heading *Food and drink* in your book.
What did children eat and drink at school 30 years ago?
What happens in your school now?

Find out how many children in your school have a hot meal at school and how many bring food from home. Write down what you find out.

Streaming

There was more competition in schools in the 1950s than there is today.

"We had marks for attendance and marks for tests. Everyone had a position in class."

Look at this school report.

Look for:

— the number in class
— the attendance number
— the different subjects
— the teacher's comments

Name Stephen Attmore	Class 3A1		Number in Class 39
Position in Exam 36	Attendance 369		Times Late

Subject	Marks Poss.	Marks Obt.	Grade	Teachers' Comments
Arithmetic:				
(a) Mental	20	17		} Very good progress
(b) Mechanical ...	40	38		} has been made.
(c) Problems	40	33		
English:				
(a) Comprehension	20	20		} Very good work has
(b) Composition	40	37		} been done in this subject
(c) Spelling	10	9½		} Compositions are
(d) General	30	22½		} always interesting.
(e) Spoken				
TOTAL ...	200	177		
History			V.G.	} Shows lively interest,
Geography			G.	} especially in Nature
Nature Study or Science ...			V.G.	} Study. Has done very
Scripture...			V.G.	} good written work & illustrations
Art			G.	
Craft or Needlework ...			G.	Has worked well.
Music			G.	Has shown great keenness.
Physical Training			V.G.	Very keen & alert.

Grading: **V.G.**—Very Good; **G.**—Good; **Av.**—Average; **W.**—Weak; **U.**—Unsatisfactory.

GENERAL REMARKS:—

Stephen has good ability & is good, conscientious worker in all subjects.

Report received and noted: Class Teacher DRGilson

B.R. Attmore
Parent or Guardian.

Headmaster E.J. Wood

Next term begins on September 10.

Children were put into different classes called "streams". Those who did well in tests went into the A class. The other children went into the B class.

"All the classes were streamed from the first year in the Juniors. Once you were put in a class it was very unusual to change. You went up the school like that."

At the end of the fourth year all the children sat an examination. It was called the "Eleven Plus" or scholarship. Those who passed it went to one sort of school. The children who didn't pass went to another sort of school. More children failed than passed.

"My parents bought me a bike for passing the scholarship, but I wasn't as happy as they were. I went on a bus to my new school. Most of my friends went to one nearer home."

Advertisement 1951

Things to do

Make two lists in your book. Call one list *School Competition Now.*
Write down what competitions you have at school.
Call the other list *School Competition Then.*
Write down what competition was for in the 1950s.

Talk to someone who sat the "Eleven Plus" or scholarship.
What was it like?

Try to borrow some old school reports.

Lessons

All Saints School, Farnworth, Lancashire 1954

Some teachers had new ideas 30 years ago.
They wanted the children to work on their own
for some of the time.

14

Look at this photograph of a school shop.
These children are learning mathematics in a new way.
The teacher is nowhere in sight.

Look for:

— the boxes and tins collected by the class
— the boy who is being shopkeeper
— the customers in the queue
— the girl and boy with the box of chocolates.

The children were taught different subjects.
Each subject had a time on the timetable.

"Mental arithmetic every morning, with always some formal English to follow. History and geography were separate subjects. We read a chapter in a book."

Things to do

Talk to someone who sat the "Eleven Plus" or scholarship. What was it like?
What were the old ideas? What were the new ones?
Write down what they tell you in your book.

What sort of lessons do you have today?

Draw a picture of a mathematics lesson 30 years ago.

Music, art and craft

London 1952

"On Fridays we had percussion band. The teacher said,
'Keep your eyes on the conductor.' If one person
played too soon, it was spoilt for all the rest."

Look at this photograph of children playing musical instruments.

Look for:

—the boy who is being the conductor
—the triangles
—the two girls with different instruments.
Can you find the boy who will make a mistake?

The new schools had sinks in the classrooms. More painting was possible in schools in the 1950s. Craft was often called handwork or handicraft. Models had to be carefully measured.

"Once a week we had craft. Boys and girls were taught separately. Boys learnt to use tools and a ruler. They made models of card and wood. Girls turned their hands to needlework."

Brockley Road School, London 1951

Things to do

Ask someone older than 30 about music lessons when they were your age.
What instruments did they play? What tunes do they remember?
Write down what they tell you in your book.

Draw a picture of the girls' sewing class.

Do you think girls and boys should learn different things?
Write down your answer in your book.

PE and dance

**"It seemed so big at first. I made myself climb
a bit higher each week till I reached the top."**

These children are
swinging on the apparatus.
They have changed their
clothes for PE. This was
all new in the 1950s.
When their mothers and
fathers went to school,
there was very little
PE equipment.

**"We wanted them all to have plimsolls.
We didn't want ordinary shoes on the new floor."**

"Country dancing was always popular. 'Rufty Tufty', 'Gathering Peascods' and 'Durham Reel' were those I liked best. The teacher called out above the music to remind us of what to do next."

George Eliot School, London 1953

The music was played on a piano or came from a record. Sometimes they had country dancing as one of the lessons. Sometimes it was after school.

Things to do

Find out about PE lessons by talking to someone who was at school 30 years ago. Then talk to someone who was at school 60 years ago. Write down what they tell you in your book.

Draw some pictures to show the differences.

Ask your teacher to let you try country dancing.

Other sports

St Francis de Sales School, London

Children at a new school in the 1950s played sports and games
on the field behind their school. Those at older schools went
to a field nearby to play.

**"There were teams for every sport. Most people had
a chance to play in something while they were at the school.
My school won the Junior Schools' Shield several times."**

"We started the annual sports day in 1952. Everyone had a lot of fun. It was quite a novelty then to have the mothers taking part."

Below is a photograph of mothers racing at a school sports.

Above and left: Arbury School, Cambridge 1960

Look for:

— the women's dresses
— the petticoat worn by one mother
— the woman wearing trousers.

Things to do

Look at the team photographs. There is one here and one on the back cover. Is the kit they wore the same as teams wear today? What is different?

Ask your teacher to look for some old team photographs.

Write about a girl whose mother won the mothers' race.

Special days

Albrighton School, Shropshire 1953

Most schools had one or two special days a year.
Sometimes the children went out. Sometimes visitors
came in. Every school celebrated the Coronation of
Queen Elizabeth II in June 1953.

The children in this photograph took part in an Elizabethan pageant.
They dressed up like people who lived at the time of the first
Queen Elizabeth.

Look for:

— the girl who is being the Queen. She has a hoop inside her skirt.
— the boy with the fancy cloak
— the three children with their feet in the stocks. They cannot
    get out until the stocks are unlocked.

At this school, they
decided to plant
a small tree. It is
a big tree now.

ROYALTY
IN ESSEX

A SOUVENIR BOOK
FOR ESSEX CHILDREN
PRESENTED BY
THE COUNTY COUNCIL OF ESSEX
ON THE OCCASION OF THE CORONATION OF
HER MAJESTY QUEEN ELIZABETH II.
ON JUNE 2ND. 1953

Most children were given
a gift for the Coronation.
Many had Coronation mugs.
Here is a book given to
children in Essex.

Things to do

Ask someone older than 30 to look through their photograph albums.
Have they any pictures taken at the time of the Coronation?
Ask them what they did at school on special days.

Try to borrow a Coronation mug or cup.

Perhaps your school celebrated the Queen's Silver Jubilee in 1978.
Write down what children at school did in 1953 and what you did 25 years later.

School 30 years ago

All Saints School, Farnworth, Lancashire 1954

This school play was called "The Magic Button". It was put on in 1954.
The children in the photograph have all grown up. Their own children
are at school now. This photograph is part of the history of the school.

Can you make a collection of photographs about your school?

Most towns have some housing estates and schools that were built in the 1950s.
The following New Towns were built in the 1950s. Some of them have museums.

Basildon, Essex
Bracknell, Berkshire
Corby, Northamptonshire
Crawley, Sussex
Cumbernauld, Strathclyde
Cwmbran, Gwent
East Kilbride, Strathclyde

Glenrothes, Fife
Harlow, Essex
Hatfield, Hertfordshire
Hemel Hempstead, Hertfordshire
Newton Aycliffe, County Durham
Peterlee, County Durham
Welwyn Garden City, Hertfordshire

Only a few of these towns have begun to collect photographs of their early
history. Perhaps you can help by collecting photographs and objects yourself.
